Letters To My Mum In Heaven

Mothers hold their children's hands for a short while, but their hearts forever...

Letters To My Mum In Heaven

Mothers hold their children's hands for a short while, but their hearts forever...

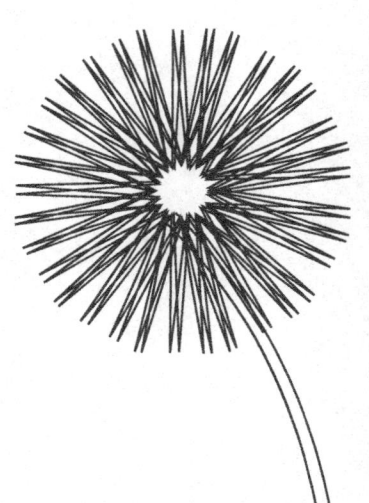

Printed in Dunstable, United Kingdom